3 8043 27105807 1

Knowsley Council

Knowsley Library Service

Please return this book on or before the date shown below

KU-072-610

You may return this book to any Knowsley library

For renewal please telephone:

Halewood 443 2086; Housebound Service / Mobile 443 4202;
Huyton 443 3734/5; Kirkby 443 4290/89;
Page Moss 443 2678; Prescot 443 5101;
School Library Service 443 4202;
Stockbridge Village 443 2501; Whiston: 426 4757

http://www.knowsley.gov.uk/

LOVE YOUR CAT

Judith Heneghan

WAYLAND

Published in 2013 by Wayland

Copyright © Wayland 2013

Wayland
338 Euston Road
London NW1 3BH

Wayland Australia
Level 17/207 Kent Street
Sydney, NSW 2000

Editor: Nicola Edwards
Designer: Rocket Design (East Anglia) Ltd
Picture researcher: Nicola Edwards

The consultant, Anna Claxton, has worked for some of the UK's largest animal welfare charities since 2003, and as a lecturer in animal welfare and animal care. She has an MSc in Applied Animal Behaviour and Animal Welfare.

British Library Cataloguing in Publication Data

Heneghan, Judith.
Love your cat. -- (Your perfect pet)
1. Cats--Juvenile literature.
I. Title II. Series
636.8-dc23
ISBN: 978 0 7502 7942 0

Printed in China

Wayland is a division of Hachette Children's Books, an Hachette UK company

www.hachette.co.uk

Picture Acknowledgements: The author and publisher would like to thank the following for allowing their pictures to be reproduced in this publication: Cover: (main) Shutterstock © Tompet, (inset) ©; title page Shutterstock © Tuboi Evgeniya; p4 iStock © SteveStone; p5 (t) Shutterstock © Faiz Zaki, (b) Shutterstock © Eric Isselée; p6 (t) Shutterstock © Sophie Bengtsson, (b) Shutterstock © Foonia; p7 iStock © Linda Kloosterhof; p8 (iStock 12091738 © Michelle Gibson; p9 (t) RSPCA Angela Hampton, (b) Shutterstock © Eric Isselée; p10 (t) Shutterstock © riekephotos, (b) iStock © Julia Mashkova; p11 (t) RSPCA Angela Hampton, (b) Shutterstock © Tompet; p12 (t) RSPCA Angela Hampton, (b) iStock 10821270 © Sharon Dominick; p13 RSPCA Geoff du Feu; p14 (t) RSPCA 1095766 Chris Brignell, (b) Shutterstock © Pavel Sazonov; p15 RSPCA 1035572 Angela Hampton; p16 (t) Shutterstock Ruth Black, (b) : iStock © khorzhevska; p17 Shutterstock © Oleg Golovnev; p18 (t) iStock 3576155 © SteveStone, (b) Shutterstock YuliaPodlenova; p19 (t) Shutterstock © Eric Isselée, (b) RSPCA Angela Hampton; p20 (t) Shutterstock © Asasirov, (b) Shutterstock © Veronika Mannova; p21 (t) Shutterstock ©Photodesign-Radloff , (b) Shutterstock © Trevor Allen; p22 (t) iStock © webphotographeer), (b) RSPCA Andrew Forsyth/RSPCA; p23 (t) RSPCA Angela Hampton, (b) iStock © collasum; p24 (t) RSCPA Andrew Forsyth/RSPCA, (b) Shutterstock © Keren-seg; p25 RSPCA Philip Toscano/RSPCA; p26 (t) Shutterstock © Aspen Photo; p27 (t) Shutterstock Igor Sokolov, (b) RSPCA 1080836 Andrew Linscott; p28 (t) Shutterstock © Tuboi Evgeniya, (b) Shutterstock © Zhuchkova Olena; p29 (t) Shutterstock © MishelVerini, (b) Shutterstock © Nailia Schwarz

KNOWSLEY LIBRARY SERVICE
271058071
Bertrams 01796363
J636.8 HALEWOOD
23·10·13

Contents

A new kitten 4
Getting ready 6
Settling in 8
Food and water 10
Keeping clean 12
Good grooming 14
Playtime! 16
On the prowl 18
Safe at home 20
Vet check 22
Going away 24
Getting older 26
Best friends 28
Quiz 30
Glossary 31
Index 32

A New Kitten

Our cat Minky came to live with us last year. We met her at the cat rescue centre. She had been abandoned, and needed a new home. They decided we could give her the care that she needed. She was only about 12 weeks old and she rubbed against my hand when I stroked her. Now she is part of our family.

Cat owners can enjoy a special bond with their pet.

The big question...

How do I choose a kitten or a cat?

A healthy cat will have clean fur, teeth and ears, clear eyes and a moist nose. A friendly cat usually enjoys being stroked or picked up, while a nervous cat might hide from you and need a quieter home. If you choose a kitten, wait until it is at least eight weeks old before taking it away from its mum.

Young kittens are very cute and playful, but each year thousands end up at cat rescue centres because their owners didn't realise how much care and attention they needed. This book will help you find out if a cat is the right pet for you.

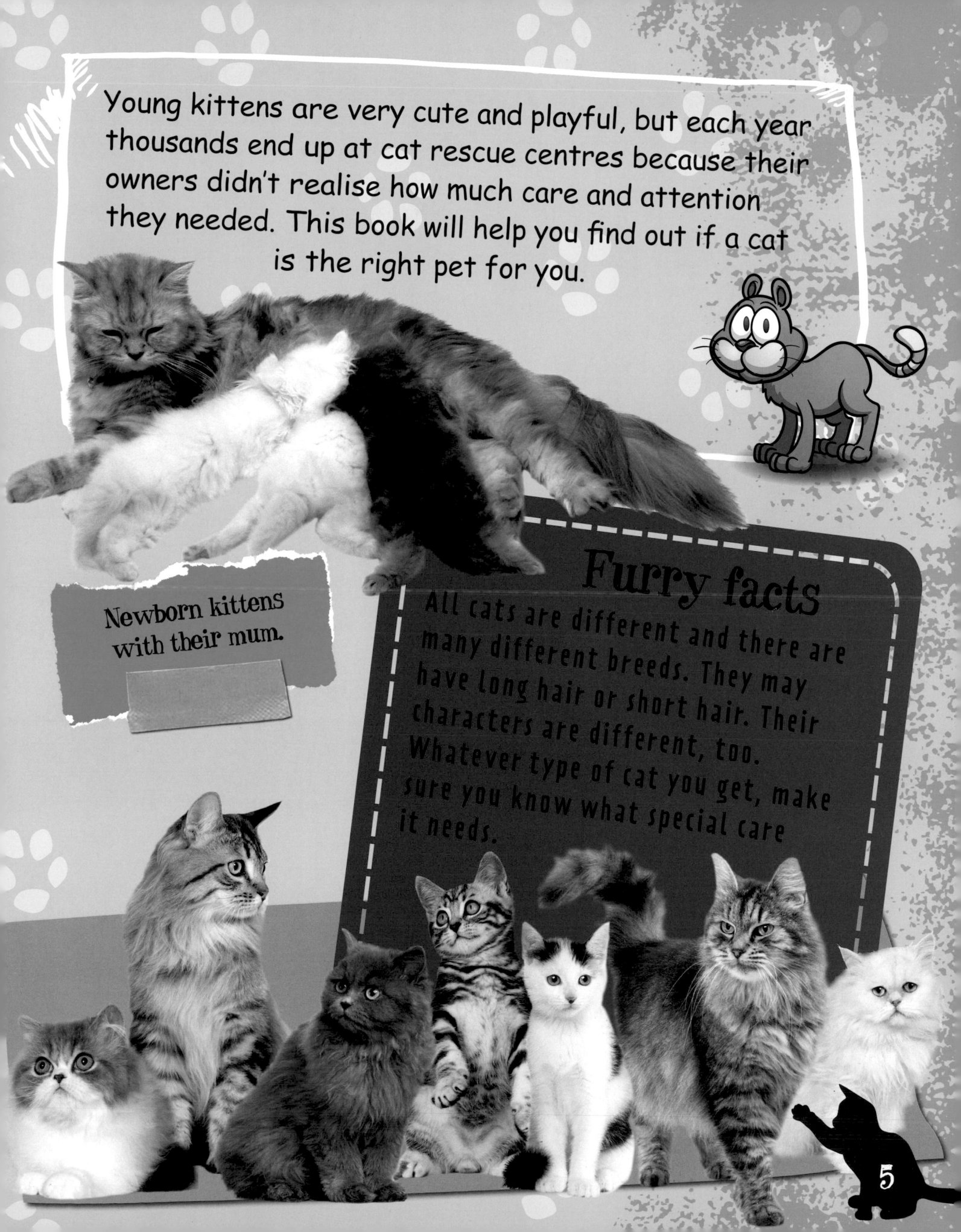

Newborn kittens with their mum.

Furry facts

All cats are different and there are many different breeds. They may have long hair or short hair. Their characters are different, too. Whatever type of cat you get, make sure you know what special care it needs.

Getting Ready

We had lots to do before we could bring Minky home. First we bought her a cosy bed with a blanket inside. I put it in a quiet corner, to help her settle in. We also bought her food bowls, a litter tray and some toys.

This cat is asleep in a warm, comfortable cat basket.

The big question...

We live in a flat. Can we have a cat?

If your cat is an 'indoor' cat you should make sure it has enough space to climb, play, jump and hide. Indoor cats still have the same needs as those that can go outside.

All cats need somewhere safe to hide when they feel frightened.

Your cat will need somewhere to go to the toilet. Most cats can be trained to use a cat litter tray, which is a tray full of special material called 'litter' that needs cleaning out and replacing every day. Just remember that your kitten may have accidents before it learns to use the tray, so be patient.

Furry facts

Cats are one of the world's most popular pets. As many as one in three families have a cat.

Settling In

Minky was a bit nervous when she first arrived. Each strange sound startled her, so we watched her while she explored and introduced new things gradually. She soon became more confident. Now her favourite place is a shelf above the kitchen radiator. She can keep an eye on everyone from there!

The big question...

Why does my cat scratch the sofa?

Cats like to scratch things as a way of saying 'I was here!' They often scratch in the same place, leaving visible scratch marks. Buy your cat a tall, sturdy scratching post. Your cat will enjoy it and it helps keep claws short too.

Scratching is normal behaviour for a cat.

Let your cat get to know you by gently stroking it, holding it and playing with it. Just remember that too many cuddles can become stressful for your cat. Leave it alone when it wants to sleep or hide.

Pet power

Cats communicate in lots of different ways. They often make a purring sound when they feel happy and relaxed. They meow to get the attention of humans. And they hiss to warn other cats to stay away!

Food and Water

The vet said Minky should have three small meals a day while she's growing. She eats cat food from the pet store and I make sure she always has a bowl of fresh water. If she doesn't eat some of her food I throw the leftovers away. She's quite fussy. She won't eat at all if her dish is too near her litter tray.

Remember to change your cat's drinking water and wash out its food bowl every day.

The big question...

Should cats drink milk?
Cats shouldn't be given cows' milk. It can make them ill. Fresh water is the only drink they need.

Cats are meat-eaters. A good quality cat food will provide them with a well-balanced diet.

Some cats are careful eaters and don't eat more than they need. However, other cats are greedy and will eat as much as you feed them. An overweight cat is much more likely to have heart and joint problems, so always give the amount of food recommended on the packaging.

Furry facts

Cats are predators. This means that in the wild, they kill smaller animals for food. They may eat several small rodents a day, which is why pet cats prefer to eat little and often.

Keeping Clean

It didn't take long to train Minky to use her litter tray. We put it somewhere quiet, away from her food bowl and her bed. We put plenty of litter inside so that she could dig around in it. If she had an accident, we put her in it straight away. The first few times she used it we gave her lots of praise. Now she knows that this is her toilet!

Cats may stop using their litter tray if you change the kind of litter you use, because it smells or feels different.

The big question...

Why won't my cat use his litter tray?

Cats like to return to the same place each time they go to the toilet. They have a powerful sense of smell, and can detect exactly where they've been before. However, they won't use a litter tray if it is too near their food or people. If your cat isn't using its litter tray, it may be ill, so speak to your vet.

Pet power

Cats may be very clean animals, but they have some smelly habits! They are territorial, which means they like to mark out their territory by spraying it with strong-smelling pee or rubbing on special scent from scent glands. This warns other cats that your cat lives there. If they do it indoors they might be stressed, so speak to your vet.

It is very important to wash your hands every time you change the litter in your cat's tray. Put the dirty litter straight into the dustbin. Cat poop contains some nasty germs that can cause serious illness.

A cat flap is a great way for your cat to go outside without having to ask.

Good Grooming

Minky isn't keen on baths, but that isn't a problem. She just licks herself clean. She sits on the windowsill and uses her tongue to wash herself in the sunshine. I groom her regularly, too.

Furry facts

Have you ever been licked by a cat? Their tongues feel surprisingly rough. This is because they are covered in tiny spikes, or barbs. As cats lick their fur, the barbs pick up any dirt and loose hairs. It's a bit like having a hairbrush on your tongue!

Cats wash their ears by licking their paws and rubbing them across their heads.

Long haired cats need to be brushed with a soft cat brush to stop them swallowing too much of their own hair. Get them used to it from a young age so that they enjoy it. Look out for fleas, too. Fleas are small biting insects that cause discomfort to your cat and to you. Luckily, protecting your cat is easy – just ask your vet for advice.

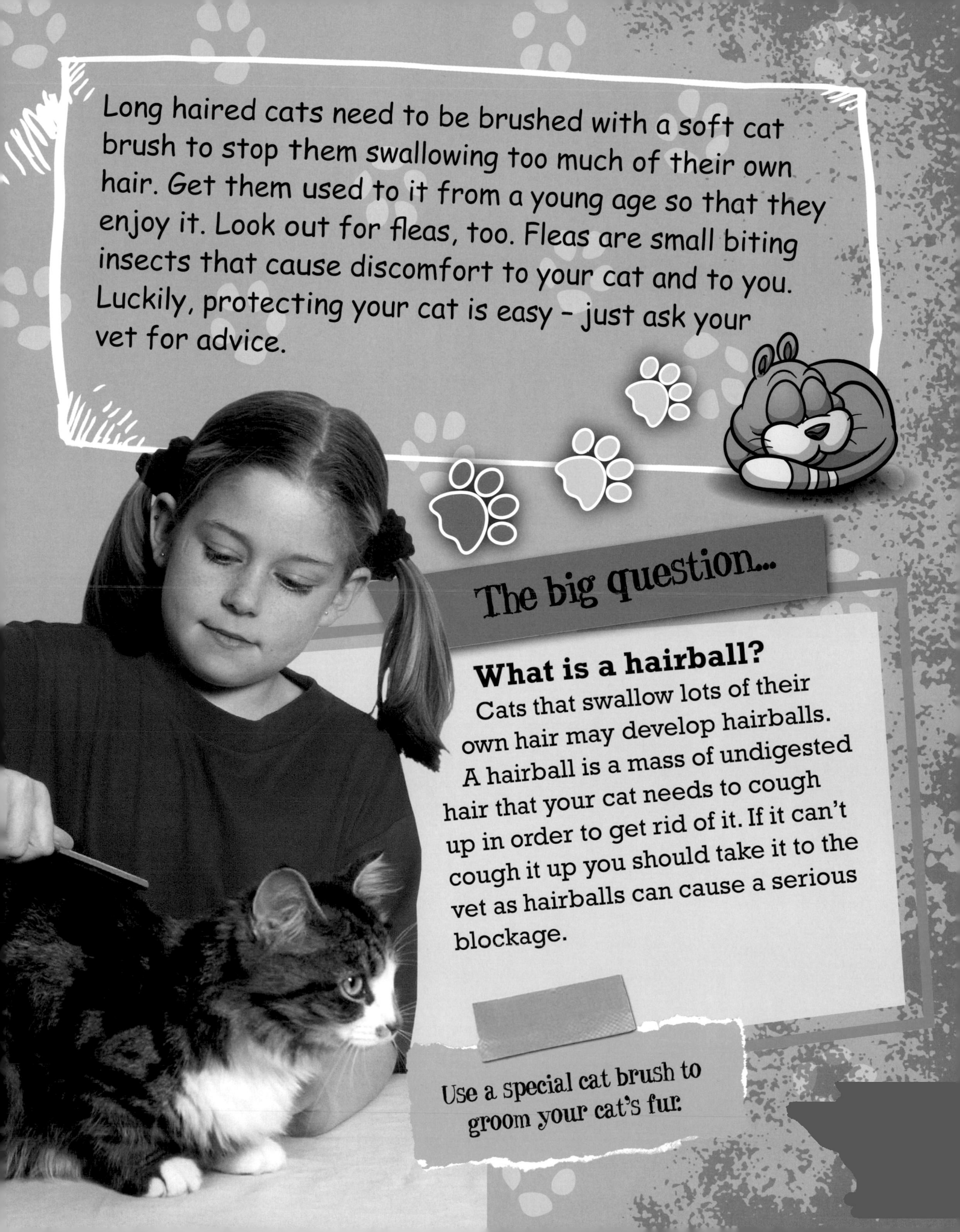

The big question...

What is a hairball?

Cats that swallow lots of their own hair may develop hairballs. A hairball is a mass of undigested hair that your cat needs to cough up in order to get rid of it. If it can't cough it up you should take it to the vet as hairballs can cause a serious blockage.

Use a special cat brush to groom your cat's fur.

Playtime!

Minky loves to play. Her favourite toy is a little cloth ball on a piece of string. If I dangle the ball in front of her, she jumps at it. If I drag it across the floor, she pounces on it and holds it between her paws. She's very fast!

Playing is good exercise for your cat, and stops them getting bored.

The big question...

What toys are best for my cat?

Cats enjoy a variety of toys they can chase, pat and bite. You don't need to spend lots of money though – a screwed up ball of paper or a stuffed sock will keep them busy. Just make sure that any toys have no loose parts that your cat might swallow or choke on.

Cats are hunters, so their bodies are built for speed and agility. Playing helps them practise their skills of running, jumping and catching. They are very good at twisting and turning too. You can put their food in a special ball to stop them getting bored as they have to work hard to get it out!

Cats use their tails to help them balance and land on their feet.

Pet power

Cats have a strong sense of curiosity, which they need to be successful hunters. When they sense something interesting they stay very still, watch carefully and prick up their ears to take in more information. Their only movement is a softly swishing tail until they are ready to get closer.

On the Prowl

Minky often hunts for mice outside. I know when she has spotted one. First she stands very still, one paw off the ground, ears pricked up. Then she makes herself as low as she can and creeps forward very quietly, until she is close enough to pounce.

The big question...

Can cats see in the dark?

Cats are especially good at spotting small movements, even in darkness. Their sensitive whiskers help, too. Whiskers detect objects such as furniture or walls by picking up tiny changes in the air. However, accidents can happen at night, so be careful if you live near a road.

This cat is stalking its prey.

Cats are territorial, which means they hunt in their own area. They don't like intruders who might take their prey. They like to patrol their patch, marking it with scent or pee to warn other cats to stay away.

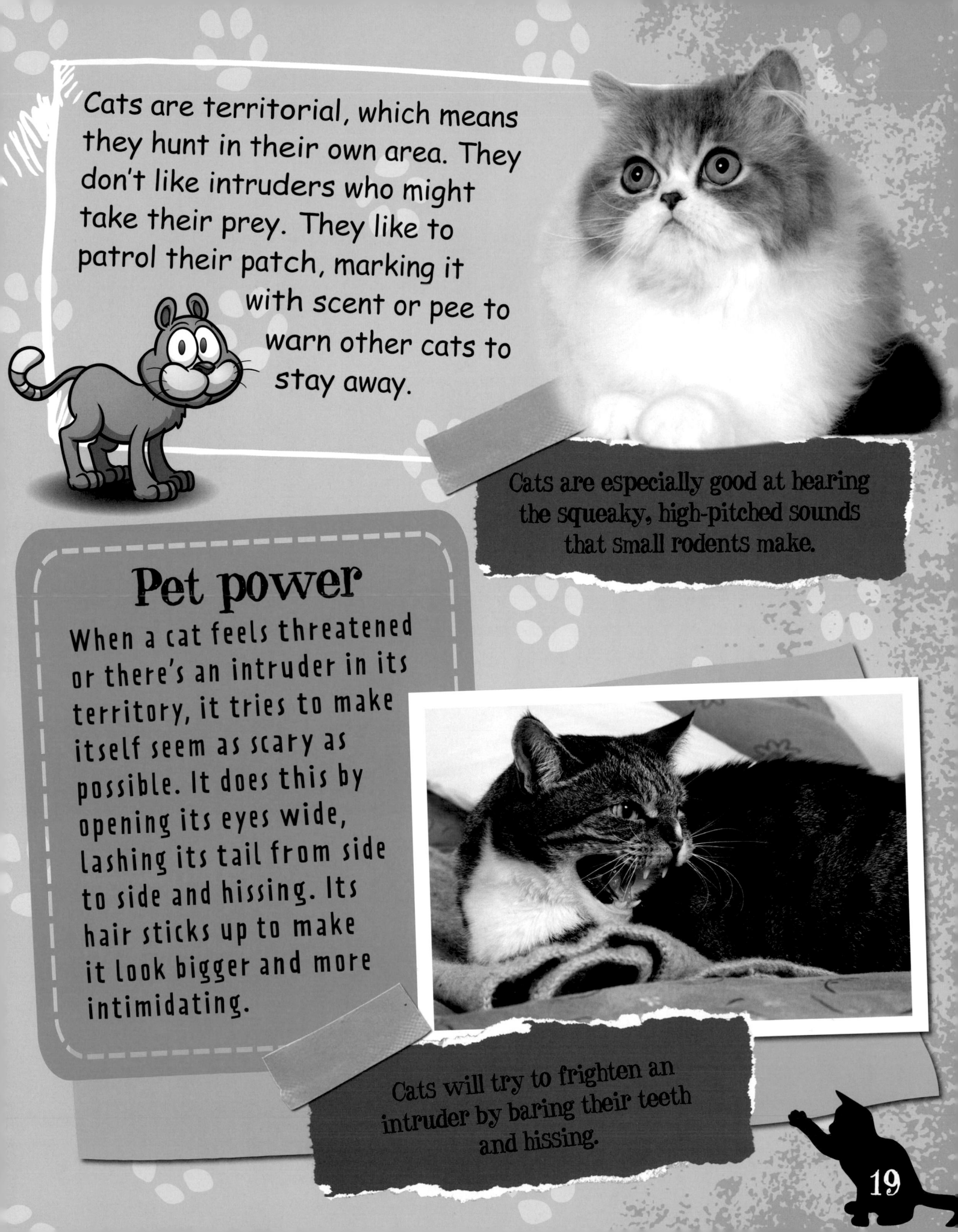

Cats are especially good at hearing the squeaky, high-pitched sounds that small rodents make.

Pet power

When a cat feels threatened or there's an intruder in its territory, it tries to make itself seem as scary as possible. It does this by opening its eyes wide, lashing its tail from side to side and hissing. Its hair sticks up to make it look bigger and more intimidating.

Cats will try to frighten an intruder by baring their teeth and hissing.

Safe at Home

Minky enjoys exploring outside, but she also loves investigating inside. Every room is a playground to her. This means we have to think about safety. Once she tried to drink out of the bath and fell straight in. Now we never leave water sitting in the bath and I must always put the toilet seat down!

The big question...

What else can I do to make our home safe for our cat?

The best way to think about safety is to imagine you are a cat. What would you climb, chew, swing from or stick your head through? Would it be dangerous? Always keep the washing machine door shut. Never leave blind cords dangling. Remember to keep a hot oven hob covered.

Remind people at home that all your appliances need to be cat-proof.

Not all hazards are obvious to humans. Did you know that some house plants are poisonous to cats? Lilies, tomato plants, daffodils and tulips are just a few of the common plants that your cat may try to nibble or play with. If these plants are eaten, your cat will become very sick and will need to be treated by a vet straight away. Never have them at home.

If you have a garden, make sure that the plants in it won't harm your cat.

Furry facts

Roads are dangerous for all animals, and road traffic accidents are the most common cause of injury or early death in cats. If you live near a busy road, think carefully about whether a pet cat will be safe and how you can protect them from harm.

If your windows face a road, keep them closed.

Vet Check

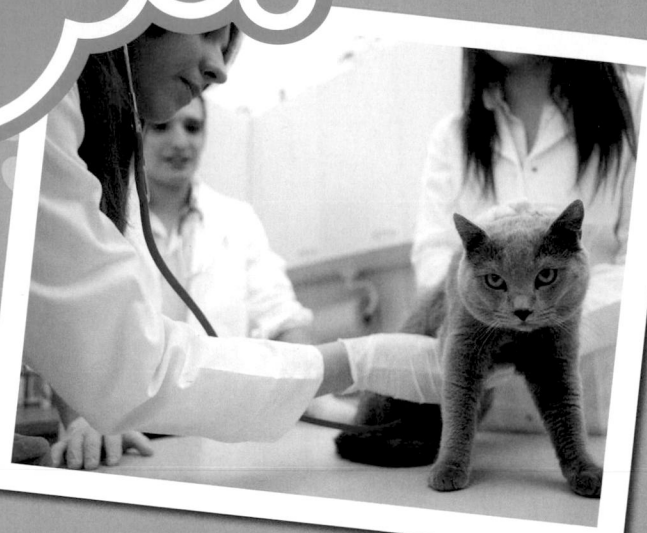

Today we took Minky to the vet for her annual check up. The vet gave her a vaccination to help stop her getting sick and examined her teeth, ears and eyes. She listened to her heart, and reminded us to give Minky tablets which stop her getting worms inside her gut.

The big question...

What is microchipping?

Microchipping is a clever way to help lost cats find their owners. First, the vet injects a microchip with its own unique number under the cat's skin. Once the chip is in place the cat can't feel it but someone using a scanner can detect it. They can then match the number to the owner's contact details which are stored on a national database.

If this cat has been microchipped, the scanner will detect it.

Cats are very good at hiding illness. Check your cat's eyes, ears, teeth and coat regularly. Look out for anything unusual such as changes in eating and drinking, weight loss or gain, soiling around the house or constant hiding. These can be signs that your cat is feeling poorly and needs to be examined by a vet.

Furry facts

Neutering is an operation to stop your cat breeding and having kittens. It is always carried out by your vet. Most experts think neutering is a good idea, because it protects your cat from disease and prevents the birth of large numbers of kittens who may not all find homes.

Check your cat's claws regularly. If they become too long, your vet may need to clip them.

Going Away

We couldn't take Minky on holiday with us. We asked our neighbours to look after her while we were away. They came in every day to feed her and play with her. I missed her, but she wouldn't have enjoyed the long car journey. She was happier at home.

Your cat may be happiest if you can get a friend or neighbour to visit them at home when you go away.

Pet power

Because cats are territorial, they like to stay on their own home ground where they feel safe and secure. They don't like change!

This cat is staying close to home.

If no one can come in to feed and play with your cat while you are away, you might decide to leave it at a cattery. Visit the cattery first to make sure it is suitable for your cat. Most catteries are happy for you to bring your cat's bed and toys with it. That way it has some familiar things to help it settle in.

The big question...

Will my cat try to run away when we move house?

Your cat may feel anxious at first, because your new home will seem strange with different smells and sounds. Your cat might try to find its way back to its old territory, so keep it indoors for two to three weeks. It should soon settle down.

Getting Older

These cats are brother and sister. They have lived together all their lives.

Minky is still quite young for a cat. My gran's old cat Duster is fifteen now. Duster still loves prowling round the garden, but he doesn't run as fast as he used to and he sleeps most of the time. He's also lost some of his teeth, so Gran has to give him softer food.

The big question...

We already have a cat. Will she mind if we get another one?

Cats get on best with other animals if they have lived together from a very young age. Your cat may get quite stressed if another cat is suddenly introduced into the house. If you have more than one cat and they don't get on, make sure they have enough space to get away from each other when they need to, as well as separate food bowls, litter trays and toys.

Cats can live for between 14 and 20 years. This is something to remember if you are thinking about getting one.

Kittens are cute, but they are a huge commitment, too. You will have to care for a cat for its whole life.

Your cat may sleep a lot more as it reaches old age.

Furry facts

Cats can sleep for up to 18 hours a day. This is because they need to save their energy for bursts of hunting and pouncing on their prey.

Best Friends

Looking after Minky is a lot of work. I have to think about all her needs – food, water, warmth and comfort, safety and health. I don't mind though – playing with her is the best fun ever and she is the warmest, cuddliest, softest animal I know.

Pet power

When a cat feels relaxed and trusting it may narrow its eyes because it isn't on the lookout for danger. A cat that lies on its back and exposes its tummy is also saying it feels safe.

A relaxed, happy cat may narrow its eyes and maybe even shut one altogether.

Some cats are more affectionate than others, but your cat is more likely to respond to you if you treat it with love and care at all times. Cats are very independent, yet can be taught to answer to their names if they trust you and feel safe with you.

Furry facts

Cats are fun to watch because they use every bit of their bodies to communicate and explore. From tails that help them keep their balance to whiskers that help them test if they can fit through a gap or under the sofa, they are truly amazing animals.

This cat shows that it trusts its owner.

Quiz

How well do you know cats?
Try this quick quiz to find out!

1. Cats are:

a. meat eaters
b. vegetarians
c. not fussy either way

2. An upright tail means your cat is feeling:

a. tall
b. hungry
c. confident

3. A territorial cat:

a. loves travelling
b. likes fighting
c. marks its home area with scent

4. Cats may meow because:

a. they've seen another cat
b. they want your attention
c. they're feeling sleepy

5. What common household items may be poisonous for your cat?

a. newspapers
b. houseplants
c. sausages

6. Cats often sleep for:

a. up to 18 hours a day
b. 24 hours a day
c. 8 hours a day

7. Cats have whiskers to:

a. protect their noses
b. look cute
c. detect objects around them

8. What does it mean if your cat rolls on its back and shows its tummy?

a. It wants you to tickle it
b. It's got a tummy ache
c. It trusts you

Answers

1(a); 2(c); 3(c); 4(b); 5(b); 6(a); 7(c); 8(c)

Glossary

abandoned left to take care of itself
annual once a year
barbs tiny rough spikes on a cat's tongue
breeds different types of cat
cat litter tray a tray that cats use to go to the toilet indoors
cattery a place that looks after cats while their owners are away
database computerised list
fleas small, jumping, blood-sucking insects
hairball a clump of undigested hair in a cat's throat or gut
hazards dangers
intimidating deliberately frightening
intruders unwelcome visitors
microchipping injecting a tiny electronic chip under the skin
neutering an operation to stop a cat breeding and having kittens
predator an animal that hunts for food
prey an animal that is hunted for food
rescue centre somewhere that looks after unwanted or abandoned animals
rodents small animals such as mice, rats and squirrels
scanner a hand-held device used to find and read microchips
scratching post an upright post covered in tough, thick material that a cat can scratch with its claws
stalking moving quietly while hunting
territorial keeping to one particular area
vaccination an injection to prevent disease

Index

attention 5

balanced diet 11
bed 6, 12, 25
behaviour 5, 8, 9, 10, 11, 16, 17, 18, 19, 24, 25, 26, 27, 29
breeds 5

care 4, 5, 28
cat flap 13
cat food 10, 11
catteries 25
characters 5
check-ups 22, 23
choosing 4
claws 23
climbing 7
communication 9

ears 4, 14, 17, 22
exercise 8, 16
exploring 8, 20
eyes 4, 19, 22

feelings 6
fleas 15
fur 4

going to the toilet 7, 12
grooming 14, 15

hair 5, 14, 15, 19
hairball 15
hazards 20, 21
hearing 19
heart 11, 22
hiding 7, 9
hissing 9, 19
holding 9
holidays 24
home alone 24, 25
hunting 17, 18, 19, 27

illness 13, 23

joints 11
jumping 7, 17

kittens 4, 5, 7, 23

learning 7, 29
litter tray 7, 10, 12, 13

marking territory 13, 19
meat-eaters 11
meowing 9
microchipping 22
moving 24

needs 28
neutering 23

old age 26, 27

paws 13, 14, 16
playing 4, 5, 7, 9, 16, 17, 20, 24, 25, 28
praise 12
predators 11
purring 9

rescue centres 4, 5

safety 6, 20, 21, 25, 29
scratching 8
sense of smell 12
sleep 6, 9, 27
stress 9, 26

tails 17, 19, 29
teeth 19, 22, 26
tongue 14
toys 16, 25
training 7, 12
trust 28, 29

vaccination 22
vet 15, 21, 22, 23

water 10, 20
weight 11
whiskers 18, 29
worms 22

The five welfare needs

In England and Wales it is the law that all pet owners must meet their pet's needs in the following way:

- a suitable place to live
- a proper diet with plenty of fresh water
- protection from and treatment of illness and injury
- allowed to behave normally
- housed with, or apart from, other animals according to their needs.

Owners who don't care for their pets in this way are breaking the law. For more information, see http://www.rspca.org.uk/allaboutanimals/pets/cats